50 THINGS TO KNOW ABOUT HOME COMPOSTING

A Beginners Guide to Learn How to Enjoy Composting Inexpensively

Catherine Lugo

50 Things to Know About Home Composting Copyright © 2018 by CZYK Publishing LLC. All Rights Reserved.

All rights reserved. No part of this book may be reproduced in any form or by any electronic or mechanical means including information storage and retrieval systems, without permission in writing from the author. The only exception is by a reviewer, who may quote short excerpts in a review.

By TimeZonesBoy (US Central Intelligence Agency) [Public domain], via Wikimedia Commons

Cover designed by:
Cover Image:

Edited by:

Greater Than a Tourist
Visit our website at www.GreaterThanaTourist.com

Lock Haven, PA
All rights reserved.

ISBN: 9781983089176

BOOK DESCRIPTION

Have you ever wondered what composting is all about?

Have you ever wondered what planet Earth is going to do with all our waste products?

Would you like to do your part to help clean up our planet?

If you answered yes to any of these questions then this book is for you...

"50 Things to Know About Home Composting" is all about the composting process; how it happens and why it's important. You'll learn about the advantages and the disadvantages of composting, how to start a compost pile of your own and about the different kinds of composting. The actual scientific process behind composting is a simple one, but the results are amazing. Starting and maintaining your home compost pile is a good family project with many lessons to teach and a way to learn more about and appreciate Mother Nature.

By the time you finish this book, you'll have the knowledge you need to produce compost that will help you grow a better garden, you'll be doing your part to help clean up our environment.

So grab YOUR copy today. You'll be glad you did.

TABLE OF CONTENTS

BOOK DESCRIPTION
TABLE OF CONTENTS
ABOUT THE AUTHOR

1. Create Compost
2. Where Did Compost Begin?
3. Reduce Your Need for Chemical Fertilizers
4. Stimulate Higher Yields of Agricultural Crops
5. Facilitate Reforestation
6. Amend Soil Problems
7. Clean up Contaminated Soil
8. Remove Storm Water Runoff Solids from Soil
9. Save on Your Water Bill
10. Balance Compost Materials
11. Break Compost up into Small Pieces
12. Water Your Compost Regularly
13. Turn your Compost Pile
14. Make Use of Worms
15. Maintain Your Worms
16. Use In-Vessel Composting
17. Green up Your Lawn
18. Choose a Structure for Holding Your Compost

19. Fix Your Compost

20. Minimize Compost Pile Pests

21. Don't Use These in Your Compost

22.

23. Produce Finished Compost

24. Control Flies in Your Compost Pile

25. Select a Spot to Compost

26. Compost Indoors

27. Build Your Own Indoor Bin

28. Teach Kids about Recycling

29. How Much Compost is needed for Decomposition?

30. Bury Organic Waste

31. Stimulate Beneficial Organisms

32. Try These Recipes

33. Keep Your Worms Happy

34. Set up Your Worm Bin

35. Give Worms a Place to Work and Rest

36. All about Worm Castings

37. Make Worm Tea

38. What the Experts Say about Worm Castings

39. What is Sheet Composting?

40. Hot Composting

41. No- Turn Cold Composting

42. How Compost Gets Hot

43. What Actinomycetes Do

44. What Fungi Can Do

45. Fauna Have a Role to Play

46. Protozoa Get in on the Act

47. The Mesophilic Stage of Composting

48. The Thermophilic Stage

49. Temperature Zonation

50. Turn Your Compost Pile

50 THINGS TO KNOW ABOUT PACKING LIGHT FOR TRAVEL

NOTES

ABOUT THE AUTHOR

Catherine Lugo has been a freelance writer for ten years. She has written various articles for the Internet as well as for print media. Her first eBook is The Dutch Oven Cookbook, available at www.smashwords.com. Her poem "Heaven Found" was published in Poetry Gems 2000; Catherine is currently at work on her first novel.

She lives in Texas with her husband and her hobbies include crafting, gardening and the study of alternative health. Catherine strives to live by what she preaches by living positively. She is a member of NAIWE, the National Association of Writers and Editors. You can contact her anytime at http://catherinelugo@naiwe.com/. Also visit her on her Amazon Author Page.

1. Create Compost

By combining organic wastes like leftover food, clippings from your yard, branches and twigs and manures from farm animals like cows or chickens, you can create your own compost. You should also add things like wood chips to speed up the breakdown of the organic materials you're using. The wood chips will help the finished material to become fully stabilized and mature all throughout the curing process. When your compost is completely mature it will have a dark brown or black component called humus.

2. Where Did Compost Begin?

The natural process we call compost has been happening since our planet began. It's a simple process of biological decomposition; plants on earth have been doing it for a long time. As vegetation from plants and trees falls to the ground and slowly decays, it provides minerals and nutrients for other plants, animals and microorganisms. You might say that compost is how the planet feeds itself. In order for compost to become mature, high temperatures are needed to kill pathogens and weed seeds that the natural decomposition process doesn't destroy.

3. Reduce Your Need for Chemical Fertilizers

Using chemical fertilizers on your lawn and plants is one way to get a greener lawn, but it's not the best thing for our environment. Over time, the use of chemical fertilizers, which are highly acidic, increases soil acidity. This, in turn, reduces beneficial organisms that live in the soil; it also can stunt the growth of plants. All of this upsets the natural ecosystem, and leads to an imbalance in Mother Nature's system as well as an imbalance in the plants themselves. Chemical fertilizer works faster than compost to provide plants the nutrition they need, but you should apply it with moderation. Too much can burn and even kill plants. Chemical fertilizers also seep into the ground water and their manufacture releases greenhouse gases into the environment.

4. Stimulate Higher Yields of Agricultural Crops

Farm composting is done on a large scale and has been shown to actually increase farm yields of agricultural crops. Farm composting is done by placing materials like manures and plant products in long trenches, sometimes as long as four miles long, two miles wide and two miles deep. The waste material is layered with each layer being moistened with water or cow dung slurry, which is basically liquefied cow manure mixed with other biodegradable farm products. Within about five to six months compost made in this way is ready for application on farm crops. Compost made this way helps the plants deal with environmental stressors and helps them absorb nutrients faster.

5. Facilitate Reforestation

It's an unfortunate fact that a lot of the organic materials in the soils of our country have been stripped away by natural and man-made stresses like erosion, flooding and logging. That's where compost comes in; it can actually restore barren soil in places like our forests and wetlands. When the missing infrastructure ingredients of soil, that soil can be rebuilt. Humus is the organic component of soil and is formed by the decomposition of leaves and other plant material. When it is added to the soil, the nutrients that plants need to reestablish themselves are put back into the soil. In this way, soil can be rebuilt.

6. Amend Soil Problems

Depending on what type of soil you have, compost can help you amend, or improve it. The three types of soil are clay, loam and sand, and you probably have some idea of what type yours is. Sometimes soil can be a mixture of one or more of these three types. Adding compost will help any kind of soil that you may have. If your soil is clay, compost will help it drain better. If your soil is sand, compost will help it hold onto moisture better. Finally, if your soil is loamy, then compost will do some of both of the above.

7. Clean up Contaminated Soil

Compost can clean up any soil you have that might be contaminated by things like hazardous materials in the environment. An example might be wood contaminants like creosote, which is a wood preservative distilled from coal tar. Heavy metals and petroleum products are two more examples of soil contaminants that compost can help clean up. The natural metabolic processes of plants and/or microorganisms found in compost can stabilize or degrade these and many other sorts of environmental contaminants. Bacteria and fungi are two of the main components of compost that will help clean up your soil.

8. Remove Storm Water Runoff Solids from Soil

Storm water runoff happens when precipitation from rain or snowmelt flows over the ground. Streets and sidewalks in our cities keep the storm water from naturally soaking into the ground. You might not think this sounds like a problem, but as the water moves along our city streets and sidewalks it picks up contaminants like chemicals, oil and grease. These substances in the water eventually flow into our lakes and rivers. These contaminants also get into our soil; this is where compost comes to the rescue once again. Add compost to your soil and it will naturally attack and remove many storm water runoff impurities.

9. Save on Your Water Bill

Water plays a major role in a healthy, good looking garden or lawn, but that doesn't mean your water bill has to be sky high. Composting your garden can help you save big on your water bill. Besides choosing native plants, using drip irrigation and mulching, compost is the smart way to save water. We Americans consume 26 billion gallons of water a day, but just a little composting can go a long way in helping reduce that number. Composting provides a natural barrier against evaporation. You'll be watering less because your plants and lawn will be able to hold onto the water you give them longer.

10. Balance Compost Materials

Materials that you use in your compost should contain things like grass clippings, food scraps and manures from animals such as cows, pigs and chickens. These are your 'green' materials and they contain a lot of nitrogen. You should also include things like dry leaves, wood chips, branches and twigs; these are your 'brown' organic materials. The 'brown' ingredients have a lot of carbon, but not very much nitrogen. The idea is to experiment with this mixture until you get the right balance. This is the part of composting that takes patience.

"It is something of a miracle to see broccoli stems, orange peels, and fallen leaves change into dark, sweet-smelling earth."

11. Break Compost up into Small Pieces

By breaking up your compost into smaller particles you will increase the surface area that on which microorganisms can feed. Consider grinding, chipping and/or shredding your compost materials. Smaller particles will also be able to mix better and improve the insulation of the pile. Better insulation means that your compost will reach the optimal temperatures needed for decomposition. Be careful not to make the particles too small; this might keep air from flowing freely within the mixture.

12. Water Your Compost Regularly

In order to keep your compost pile decomposing properly, you need to water it regularly. The water will help to transport the nutrients within the pile. Water also makes the organic material accessible to the microbes so they can better break it down. Moisture for your compost can come from you watering it yourself or from rainfall. How often you water can depend a lot on the materials in your compost; heavy materials like straw and twigs need more moisture than materials like grass clippings and manure. A good test for moisture is to grab a handful of compost and squeeze it; only a few drops of water should come out. If more comes out, your pile is too wet.

13. Turn your Compost Pile

Make sure your compost gets plenty of air; this will make decomposition happen faster. Use a pitchfork or a shovel to turn your compost every few days, but be careful not to turn it too often as this will dry it out. You can also use bulking agents like wood chips or shredded newspaper to help aerate your compost. Turn the material on the outside of the pile to the inside; the number of times you turn it will depend on the materials in the compost and its moisture content. A too moist pile will benefit from more frequent turning.

14. Make Use of Worms

Vermicomposting is another popular method of composting. Put red worms from your garden into a bin filled with organic material, like newspaper for bedding, and food scraps. The worms will break down the material into a high-value compost called castings. Your worms can live in just about any kind of bin; but a small to medium sized plastic storage bin works well. Worms will eat almost anything you put in the bin, and you can put just about anything that you would put in a compost pile. Vermicomposting is ideal for anyone who has a small amount of space, such as people who live in apartments. Some schools have vermicomposting programs to teach children about conservation and recycling.

15. Maintain Your Worms

Maintain your worms by monitoring their bin temperature. The bin temperature should never be too hot or too cold. The best temperature is in the range of 55 to 75 degrees. Never place the bin in direct sunlight, and if you live in a hot, arid climate, keep your bin in a shady spot. As long as you provide the right conditions and food, like kitchen scraps and newspaper, your worms will thrive and produce compost. One pound of mature worms, which is about 800-1000 worms, can eat up to half a pound of organic material in one day. In about three to four months, you'll have compost that you can use as potting soil. You can also make 'worm tea' from their castings; this is a high quality fertilizer for house plants or gardens.

16. Use In-Vessel Composting

In-Vessel composting uses various kinds of vessels, like drums or silos, to produce compost. You can put your organic material into a drum and more easily control the temperature, moisture and aeration it needs. Most drums or barrels used for composting have a handle you can rotate them with in order to mix the compost. In-vessel composting is a good method for small scale composting since it takes up less room and is self-contained. Another benefit of in-vessel composting is that almost any kind of organic waste can be used without fear of unwanted animal attraction.

17. Green up Your Lawn

You can use your compost as a mulch, or mix it into your soil. Mulch is any kind of material that you spread over the surface of the soil as a covering to protect it from temperature extremes and also to help it hold in moisture. Compost, when used on your lawn, provides a very reliable source of fertilizer and is also an excellent soil conditioner. The microorganisms in compost help soil by loosening it up so that it had better aeration and drainage. When you use compost on your lawn and landscaping it can help the grass hold onto water. Compost also has most of the nutrients plants need for strong, healthy growth.

18. Choose a Structure for Holding Your Compost

You can make your compost in almost any kind of structure; it's really a matter of personal preference. If you're a do it yourselfer, you can build your own bin very inexpensively. Many people build their bins out of wire, bricks, wooden pallets or concrete blocks, to name a few. But you can get as creative as you like and build one out of just about anything. You can also go to the store and buy a prefabricated bin that will work just fine. You might like a drum unit from a building supply store; these usually have a handle that you can use to turn the drum; this is the equivalent of turning your compost with a pitchfork or shovel. Look for readymade compost bins in several places; building supply stores, garden centers, catalogues and online as well. But remember, home composting doesn't have to be done in any kind of container at all.

19. Fix Your Compost

Keep an eye on your compost by trusting your nose. If your compost pile is wet and smells like a mixture of rancid butter, vinegar and rotten eggs, you can bet it needs more air. It smells rotten because it has too much 'fresh' material in it, which is putting out too much nitrogen. The way to fix this condition is to turn the pile and add dry material to it. Add things like dry leaves, wood shavings and wood chips. If the pile is very wet, then you need to provide drainage and the more dry ingredients you add, the more drainage you'll get. If it's too wet to deal with, the best thing is just to cover the entire pile with dirt and let it dry out while you start another pile.

20. Minimize Compost Pile Pests

If you see insects and larvae in your compost, it could be because you're adding the wrong ingredients. Many times, the pest problem is caused by adding meat and other animal products to your pile. You can minimize these pests by not adding meat, and by keeping the temperature of your compost high. As soon as you get your pile built, you should allow it to 'bake. It should heat quickly and reach the desired temperature of 90 to 140 degrees Fahrenheit. This should take about four to five days; stirring and turning it as it bakes speeds up the decomposition process. If your pile is too small, it won't heat up as fast as it should, so make sure you have a sizeable pile to start off with.

"Composting appeals to the thrifty person in all of us. It feels good to keep materials on site and cycle them back into the yard and garden."

21. Don't Use These in Your Compost

Don't use things like meat, fat, pet droppings, milk, bones, diseased plants, weeds, cheese or oil of any kind. If you use these kinds of products, you'll attract all kinds of animals to your pile. This will create an unwanted pest problem at your home. If you used sick plants or weeds in your compost, they will spread disease back into your soil when you use your compost later. The best materials to use are kitchen leftovers, like potato skins and vegetable waste, and yard waste, like grass clippings. Chop or shred these materials for faster decomposition.

22. Conserve Nitrogen in Your Compost

The major nutrient components of organic materials are nitrogen (N), phosphorus (P), and potash (K). Of all of these three, nitrogen conservation is the most important. In your compost pile, nitrogen will be the one nutrient that is the easiest lost. Nitrogen leaches out of the compost in the form of ammonia or other gases. Some ways that nitrogen can be lost is through the moisture content, aeration and temperature. High temperatures, as in hot and arid climates, will cause ammonia to escape more readily; try to avoid compost temperatures above 170 degrees.

23. Produce Finished Compost

There is really no time exact time period for 'finished' compost; your compost pile may never be total, perfect or done. Compost is, by its very nature, a work in progress. There is a current rule of thumb when it comes to how long it takes compost to become usable, and that time is usually about one year. Most composting methods will take about one year and there are some methods that can take up to two years. Factors like the kind of organic material used, temperatures inside and outside the pile and the balance of brown and green materials all make a difference in how long it takes your compost to be usable.

24. Control Flies in Your Compost Pile

One of the most common pests of the compost pile is flies; and controlling them is one of your most important considerations. Flies, including the everyday housefly, can spend their larval phase as maggots inside your pile. Though they can play an important role in the breaking down of all types of organic debris, they are still unwanted guests around your household. Things like garbage, livestock manure and food scraps attract flies and then they begin breeding and developing. By shredding your compost material into pieces no larger than 2 inches, and by turning the material frequently, you can help discourage their breeding.

25. Select a Spot to Compost

Backyard composting is fun and easy. If you have a shady spot in your backyard, that's the best spot to begin your pile. The spot should also be dry and close to a water source so that you can keep your pile moist, but also so that the pile won't get too damp. Add your brown and green matter to your pile and make sure that both are shredded or chopped into small pieces; as you add these pieces, moisten them somewhat. You shouldn't drench them so that the pile can't dry out, but sprinkle water on them as you go. This is a good beginning to your backyard compost pile.

26. Compost Indoors

Composting indoors is easier than you might think, and a great idea if you don't have room outside. You'll need a special type of bin that you can buy at a hardware store, a gardening supply store or make yourself. If you tend your pile and keep track of all that you put in it, there will be no unwanted smells or pests to worry about. This will most likely produce a much smaller amount of compost, but it should be ready for you to use in about two to five weeks.

27. Build Your Own Indoor Bin

Buy two plastic garbage cans, one large and one somewhat smaller. There are several sizes of garbage cans available; the size you choose will depend on how much compost you want or need to make. Drill half inch holes in the bottom and sides of the larger can. Then put a brick in the bottom of the larger can and surround it with something like wood chips or wood shavings or even soil. Place the smaller garbage can inside on top of the brick and wood chips. Next, wrap the larger can with some kind of insulation, like plastic; this will keep the compost warm and dry. Now all you have to do is begin filling your compost bin with organic matter. Put the lid on to help keep pests out.

28. Teach Kids about Recycling

Composting, either in the classroom or somewhere outside on the school grounds is a great way to teach kids about reducing and recycling biodegradable wastes. Kids can watch the process of organic wastes turning into usable compost right before their very eyes. Be sure kids wear dust masks and gloves when they work around compost to help prevent any kind of infection. If the compost pile is outside, keep it away from any windy areas that might blow contaminants onto children. Show kids how to tend the compost pile by turning it; also teach about good hygiene when working with compost.

29. How Much Compost is needed for Decomposition?

A large compost pile will insulate itself better than a small one. It will hold the heat of microbial activity, and its center will be warmer than the edges. Piles that are smaller than 27 cubic feet will have trouble holding in the heat needed for decomposition. On the other hand, piles larger than 125 cubic feet won't allow enough air to reach the microbes inside the center of the pile. So you should work at getting your pile the right size for maximum decomposition.

30. Bury Organic Waste

A very simple method of composting is to bury your organic waste at least eight inches below the surface of the ground. A post hole digger is an excellent tool for digging the holes. After you fill the holes with organic waste like kitchen scraps and grass clippings, just cover the hole up and mark the spot so you can find it again next season. When you dig it up, you should have rich compost to use. The problem with this method is that rodents, dogs and wild animals might get to your compost first. You can also use this method near shrubs and trees that need extra nutrients, or in your garden.

"Build and maintain a compost pile if you want to become a better gardener. "

31. Stimulate Beneficial Organisms

Compost is just full of all kinds of beneficial microorganisms and soil fauna. These little beings help convert nutrients in the soil into a usable substance that can be absorbed easily by your plants. Besides microorganisms there are enzymes, vitamins and natural antibiotics in your compost that will actually go to battle for your plants and keep pathogens from harming them. Compost also has macroorganisms like earthworms and millipedes that tunnel through the compost and make it possible for air and water to reach the inside of your pile.

32. Try These Recipes

Your compost will work the best when you balance the carbon rich and nitrogen rich materials in it. The ratio should be 25:1 (brown to green). Put lots of high carbon materials in, these are brown things like straw, dry leaves and wood chips, and a lesser amount of green things like kitchen scraps and grass clippings. Too much carbon and not enough nitrogen means that your pile will decompose very slowly because there won't be enough for the microbes to eat; the pile will also be soggy and have a bad smell. But don't worry about being exact, just use about three times as much brown as you do green.

33. Keep Your Worms Happy

Composting with worms, vermicomposting, is one of the easiest ways to get compost in smaller amounts. All kinds of worms are real go getters when it comes to making compost; the most popular type are red worms (also known as red wigglers), manure worms and branding worms. Branding worms are the smaller ones usually sold by commercial breeders. If you decide to try your hand at vermicomposting, you should know that worms love kitchen scraps and hate heat. You must keep them away from high temperatures or they'll die very quickly. Just remember to keep your worm bin in a place where the temperature is between 50 and 80 degrees.

34. Set up Your Worm Bin

Set up your worm bin well before your worms arrive. One pound of worms can fit easily into one square foot of space, but since worms multiply quickly, it's probably better to start out with half a pound of worms to one square foot of space. The bin you set up for them should allow them to have 8-10 inches of bedding and compost. Drill holes in the top of your bin about every two inches; drill several holes in the bottom of the bin too. Place a drip pan underneath the bin to catch any leachate, and elevate the entire bin on bricks or blocks of wood to allow for air circulation.

35. Give Worms a Place to Work and Rest

The bottom working layer of your bin should 4-6 inches of moist, half-decomposed compost; on top of this put one handful of sand. The top layer, which is the resting layer, should have 4-6 inches of moist bedding-a good carbon source. Use something like shredded newspaper, shredded cardboard, hay, straw or leaves. All of these are organic materials. The moisture of your worm bin should have the same amount of moisture as a wrung out sponge. After you have all of these layers in your bin, let it rest for about two weeks. During this time. The compost can 'cool' and the microbes will begin to work on decomposing.

36. All about Worm Castings

Worm castings are nothing more than worm poop; and you're gonna love what they do for your garden. The castings are chock full of plant nutrients. Trace minerals and growth enhancers. Using them in your garden soil will greatly increase the good microbial activity in the root zone of your plants; where they need it most. Worm castings won't burn plants and their consistency is close to that of peat. Work your castings into your garden soil or into landscaping to improve soil structure and increase moisture.

37. Make Worm Tea

You can make a worm tea from worm leachate that is super good for your plants. Worm tea can protect plants from various kinds of infections and attack by pathogenic organisms. If a plant has been exposed to pesticides, you can use the tea as a root wash to reintroduce the microbes that the pesticide may have killed. Take 2 cups of well composted worm castings, 2 tablespoons of corn syrup or unsulphured molasses; mix it with water that has been standing overnight or rainwater. Add the molasses or corn syrup to the water, and put the worm castings into some kind of netting and place it into the water solution. Let it sit for 24 hours and stir often. Use this mix within 48 hours and apply the tea in a 1:5 ratio, on part tea to five parts water, once a week.

38. What the Experts Say about Worm Castings

Worm castings have at least 5 times the available nitrogen, 7 times the available potash and 1 ½ times more calcium than that found in   cm of the best top soil. The nutrients that castings provide your plants are water soluble and immediately ready for plants to use. Most potting soils have a nutrient life of 2-5 days, however, worm castings have been shown to last up to 6 times longer. So you need 5 times as much potting soil to so the same job as a much smaller amount of worm castings. In the long run, you'll save money on potting soil by using your worm castings.

39. What is Sheet Composting?

When you do sheet composting, you spread organic material out on the surface of the soil or untilled ground and just let it decompose. Over time, the material will slowly work its way back into the soil. This method of composting is good for forage land, no-till applications, erosion control and roadside landscaping. When this type of composting is done, you'll have more weed seeds, pathogens and fly larvae, so you should only use plants and manure in your compost. The length of time for decomposition will vary a lot depending on weather conditions, and may take a long time.

40. Hot Composting

Hot composting is the fastest way to produce good compost. It's the fastest method and it also kills off things like fly larvae and weed seeds more reliably. The disadvantage of hot composting is that it requires more management and hands on work. You'll need a compost thermometer and will have to turn the pile every 4-7 days, or whenever the pile temperature gets near 110 degrees. This method will produce good compost in about one month. Cold composting.

Compost is simply Mother Nature's way of recycling.

41. No- Turn Cold Composting

This method of composting takes anyw months to a year. You can put this pile in a shady spot; you don't need to expose it to the sun. There is also no need to worry about your mixture of green and brown, just throw stuff like kitchen waste and leaves on as you have the time. Don't worry too much about the size of your particles, cold composting is the laid back gardener's way to build a pile. Just keep adding to it as you have materials, and nature will take care of the rest.

42. How Compost Gets Hot

Bacteria are the heating and decomposing agents of compost. Of the billions of microorganisms found in one gram of compost, 80-90 % of them are bacteria. They come in lots of varieties and they use enzymes to break down the elements of waste in your compost. Bacteria are single-celled and are shaped like rods, spheres and spirals and can move on their own. As the compost heats up, a type of bacteria called thermophilic take over. Bacteria can thrive in compost unless conditions become unfavorable, then they enclose themselves in thick walled spores resistant to heat, cold, dryness or lack of food.

43. What Actinomycetes Do

These little microorganisms are the ones that give soil its characteristic earthy smell. They look like fungi but are really filamentous bacteria. Their role in the compost pile is to break down complex fibers like cellulose, lignin and proteins. They also have enzymes that can break down tough debris like wood and bark. Actinomycetes form long, thread-like filaments that look like spider webs snaking through your compost pile. You'll see them near the final stages of decomposition in your compost pile.

44. What Fungi Can Do

Fungi include molds and yeasts and in the world of your compost pile they're responsible for the decomposition of many complex plant polymers. They can break down tough debris and so allow bacteria to continue the decomposition process. When temperatures are high, fungi live in the outer layers of your compost pile and can look like grey and white fuzzy colonies.

45. Fauna Have a Role to Play

The fauna of your compost pile include creatures like millipedes and centipedes. They grind your compost up into even smaller bits so that it's easier for them to decompose; this process is known as communition. Fauna also increase the surface area to volume ratio. By doing this, fauna increase the access the microbes have to organic substrates. The substrate is the surface on which the microorganisms live. If there is more surface, the microorganisms can make more compost.

46. Protozoa Get in on the Act

Protozoa are the microorganisms that are very active in the early stages of the compost process. Their main job is to process smaller bits of organic material. By preying on the microbial populations in the compost pile, they regulate their numbers and recycle nutrients. Protozoa are a very diverse group of microorganisms and include such things as flagellates and amoebas. They are one celled and can move on their own; they have a nucleus and are larger than bacteria.

47. The Mesophilic Stage of Composting

Bacteria and fungi are very common players in this stage of compost, but fauna and protozoa are also present and play an important role. During this phase, the decomposition of things like sugars, proteins and starches takes place. Because of all this decomposition, heat begins to be generated and the decomposition process is started.

48. The Thermophilic Stage

During this stage of the process the heat-loving bacteria like actinomycetes and fungi take over as the main players. Any organisms that can't stand heat will either be destroyed or go dormant. These high temperatures will begin the breaking down process of proteins, fats and complex polymers. A polymer is any substance that has a molecular structure consisting mostly of a number of units bonded together. Plants are made of a polymer called cellulose.

49. Temperature Zonation

Temperatures in the center of your pile can go as high as 150 degrees. In the center of the pile is where the most heat resistant bacteria live. The edges of the pile will be cooler and here is where the thermophilic bacteria, actinomycetes and fungi live. They all play a part in an active, healthy compost pile.

50. Turn Your Compost Pile

Turning your compost pile will accomplish many things. It will redistribute microorganisms and cool the pile so that it doesn't get too hot and kill off too many microorganism. Both of these actions are very important for a healthy compost pile. Turning the pile will let air get into the pile and this will speed up the decomposition process. Then the entire compost process will be able to begin again and eventually turn into usable compost for your garden.

Bonus Book

50 THINGS TO KNOW ABOUT PACKING LIGHT FOR TRAVEL

Pack the Right Way Every Time

Author: Manidipa Bhattacharyya

First Published in 2015 by Dr. Lisa Rusczyk. Copyright 2015. All Rights Reserved. No part of this publication may be reproduced, including scanning and photocopying, or distributed in any form or by any means, electronic or mechanical, or stored in a database or retrieval system without prior written permission from the publisher.

Disclaimer: The publisher has put forth an effort in preparing and arranging this book. The information provided herein by the author is provided "as is". Use this information at your own risk. The publisher is not a licensed doctor. Consult your doctor before engaging in any medical activities. The publisher and author disclaim any liabilities for any loss of profit or commercial or personal damages resulting from the information contained in this book.

Edited by Melanie Howthorne

Introduction

He who would travel happily
must travel light.

-Antoine de Saint-Exupéry

Travel takes you to different places from seas and mountains to deserts and much more. In your travels you get to interact with different people and their cultures. You will, however, enjoy the sights and interact positively with these new people even more, if you are travelling light.

When you travel light your mind can be free from worry about your belongings. You do not have to spend precious vacation time waiting for your luggage to arrive after a long flight. There is be no chance of your bags going missing and the best part is that you need not pay a fee for checked baggage.

People who have mastered this art of packing light will root for you to take only one carry-on, wherever you go. However, many people can find it really hard to pack light. More so if you are travelling with children. Differentiating between "must have" and "just in case" items is the starting point. There will be ample shopping avenues at your destination which are just waiting to be explored.

This book will show you 'packing' in a new 'light' – pun intended – and help you to embrace light packing practices for all of your future travels.

Off to packing!

Dedication

I dedicate this book to all the travel buffs that I know, who have given me great insights into the contents of their backpacks.

About The Author

Manidipa Bhattacharyya is a creative writer and editor, with an education in English literature and Linguistics. After working in the IT industry for seven long years she decided to call it quits and follow her heart instead. Manidipa has been ghost writing, editing, proof reading and doing secondary research services for many story tellers and article writers for about three years. She stays in Kolkata, India with her husband and a busy two year old. In her own time Manidipa enjoys travelling, photography and writing flash fiction.

Manidipa believes in travelling light and never carries anything that she couldn't haul herself on a trip. However, travelling with her child changed the scenario. She seemed to carry the entire world with her for the baby on the first two trips. But good sense prevailed and she is again working her way to becoming a light traveler, this time with a kid.

The Right Travel Gear

1. Choose Your Travel Gear Carefully

While selecting your travel gear, pick items that are light weight, durable and most importantly, easy to carry. There are cases with wheels so you can drag them along – these are usually on the heavy side because of the trolley. Alternatively a backpack that you can carry comfortably on your back, or even a duffel bag that you can carry easily by hand or sling across your body are also great options. Whatever you choose, one thing to keep in mind is that the luggage itself should not weigh a ton, this will give you the flexibility to bring along one extra pair of shoes if you so desire.

2. Carry The Minimum Number Of Bags

Selecting light weight luggage is not everything. You need to restrict the number of bags you carry as well. One carry-on size bag is ideal for light travel. Most carriers allow one cabin baggage plus one purse, handbag or camera bag as long as it slides under the seat in front. So technically, you can carry two items of luggage without checking them in.

3. Pack One Extra Bag

Always pack one extra empty bag along with your essential items. This could be a very light weight duffel bag or even a sturdy tote bag which takes up minimal space. In the event that you end up buying a lot of souvenirs, you already have a handy bag to stuff all that into and do not have to spend time hunting for an appropriate bag.

I'm very strict with my packing and have everything in its right place. I never change a rule. I hardly use anything in the hotel room. I wheel my own wardrobe in and that's it.

Charlie Watts

Clothes & Accessories

4. Plan Ahead

Figure out in advance what you plan to do on your trip. That will help you to pick that one dress you need for the occasion. If you are going to attend a wedding then you have to carry formal wear. If not, you can ditch the gown for something lighter that will be comfortable during long walks or on the beach.

5. Wear That Jacket

Remember that wearing items will not add extra luggage for your air travel. So wear that bulky jacket that you plan to carry for your trip. This saves space and can also help keep you warm during the chilly flight.

6. Mix and Match

Carry clothes that can be interchangeably used to reinvent your look. Find one top that goes well with a couple of pairs of pants or skirts. Use tops, shirts and jackets wisely along with other accessories like a scarf or a stole to create a new look.

7. Choose Your Fabric Wisely

Stuffing clothes in cramped bags definitely takes its toll which results in wrinkles. It is best to carry wrinkle free, synthetic clothes or merino tops. This will eliminate the need for that small iron you usually bring along.

8. Ditch Clothes Pack Underwear

Pack more underwear and socks. These are the things that will give you a fresh feel even if you do not get a chance to wear fresh clothes. Moreover these are easy to wash and can be dried inside the hotel room itself.

9. Choose Dark Over Light

While picking your clothes choose dark coloured ones. They are easy to colour coordinate and can last longer before needing a wash. Accidental food spills and dirt from the road are less visible on darker clothes.

10. Wear Your Jeans

Take only one pair of Jeans with you, which you should wear on the flight. Remember to pick a pair that can be worn for sightseeing trips and is equally eloquent for dinner. You can add variety by adding light weight cargoes and chinos.

11. Carry Smart Accessories

The right accessory can give you a fresh look even with the same old dress. An intelligent neck-piece, a couple of bright scarves, stoles or a sarong can be used in a number of ways to add variety to your clothing. These light weight beauties can double up as a nursing cover, a light blanket, beach wear, a modesty cover for visiting places of worship, and also makes for an enthralling game of peek-a-boo.

12. Learn To Fold Your Garments

Seasoned travellers all swear by rolling their clothes for compact and wrinkle free packing. Bundle packing, where you roll the clothes around a central object as if tying it up, is also a popular method of compact and wrinkle free packing. Stacking folded clothes one on top of another is a big no-no as it makes creases extreme and they are difficult to get rid of without ironing.

13. Wash Your Dirty Laundry

One of the ways to avoid carrying loads of clothes is to wash the clothes you carry. At some places you might get to use the laundry services or a Laundromat but if you are in a pinch, best solution is to wash them yourself. If that is the plan then carrying quick drying clothes is highly recommended, which most often also happen to be the wrinkle free variety.

14. Leave Those Towels Behind

Regular towels take up a lot of space, are heavy and take ages to dry out. If you are staying at hotels they will provide you with towels anyway. If you are travelling to a remote place, where the availability of towels look doubtful, carry a light weight travel towel of viscose material to do the job.

15. Use A Compression Bag

Compression bags are getting lots of recommendation now days from regular travellers. These are useful for saving space in your luggage when you have to pack bulky dresses. While packing for the return trip, get help from the hotel staff to arrange a vacuum cleaner.

Footwear

16. Put On Your Hiking Boots

If you have plans to go hiking or trekking during your trip, you will need those bulky hiking boots. The best way to carry them is to wear them on flight to save space and luggage weight. You can remove the boots once inside and be comfortable in your socks.

17. Picking The Right Shoes

Shoes are often the bulkiest items, along with being the dainty if you are a female. They need care and take up a lot of space in your luggage. It is advisable therefore to pick shoes very carefully. If you plan to do a lot of walking and site seeing, then wearing a pair of comfortable walking shoes are a must. For more formal occasions you can carry durable, light weight flats which will not take up much space.

18. Stuff Shoes

If you happen to pack a pair of shoes, ensure you utilize their hollow insides. Tuck small items like rolled up socks or belts to save space. They will also be easy to find.

Toiletries
19. Stashing Toiletries

Carry only absolute necessities. Airline rules dictate that for one carry-on bag, liquids and gels must be in 3.4 ounce (100ml) bottles or less, and must be packed in a one quart zip-lock bag. If you are planning to stay in a hotel, the basic things will be provided for you. It's best is to buy the rest from the local market at your destination.

20. Take Along Tampons

Tampons are a hard to find item in a lot of countries. Figure out how many you need and pack accordingly. For longer stays you can buy them online and have them delivered to where you are staying.

21. Get Pampered Before You Travel

Some avid travellers suggest getting a pedicure and manicure just the day before travelling. This not only gives you a well kept look, you also save the trouble of packing nail polish. Remember, every little bit of weight reduced adds up.

Electronics
22. Lugging Along Electronics

Electronics have a large role to play in our lives today. Most of us cannot imagine our lives away from our phones, laptops or tablets. However while travelling, one must consider the amount of weight these electronics add to our luggage. Thankfully smart phones come along with all the essentials tools like a camera, email access, picture editing tools and more. They are smart to the point of eliminating the need to carry multiple gadgets. Choose a smart phone that suits all your requirements and travel with the world in your palms or pocket.

23. Reduce the Number of Chargers

If you do travel with multiple electronic devices, you will have to bear the additional burden of carrying all their chargers too. Check if a single charger can be used for multiple devices. You might also consider investing in a pocket charger. These small devices support multiple devices while keeping you charged on the go.

24. Travel Friendly Apps

Along with smart phones come numerous apps, which are immensely helpful in our travels. You name it and you have an app for it at hand – take pictures, sharing with friends and family, torch to light dark roads, maps, checking flight/train times, find hotels and many other things. Use these smart alternatives to traditional items like books to eliminate weight and save space.

I get ideas about what's essential when packing my suitcase.

-Diane von Furstenberg

Travelling With Kids

25. Bring Along the Stroller

Kids might enjoy walking for a while but they soon tire out and a stroller is the just the right thing for them to rest in while you continue your tour. Strollers also double duty as a luggage carrier and shopping bag holder. Remember to pick a light weight, easy to handle brand of stroller. Better yet, find out in advance if you can rent a stroller at your destination.

26. Bring Only Enough Diapers for Your Trip

Diapers take up a lot of space and add to the weight of your luggage. Therefore it is advisable to carry just enough diapers to last through the trip and a few for afterwards, till you buy fresh stock at your destination. Unless of course you are travelling to a really remote area, in which case you have no choice but to carry the load. Otherwise diapers are something you will find pretty easily.

27. Take Only A Couple Of Toys

Children are easily attracted by new things in their environment. While travelling they will find numerous 'new' objects to scrutinize and play with. Packing just one favorite toy is enough, or if there is no favorite toy leave out all of them in favor of stories or imaginary games.

28. Carry Kid Friendly Snacks

Create a small snack counter in your bag to store away quick bites for those sudden hunger pangs. Depending on the child's age this could include chocolates, raisins, dry fruits, granola bars or biscuits. Also keep a bottle of water handy for your little one. These things do not add much weight and can be adjusted in a handbag or knapsack.

29. Games to Carry

Create some travel specific, imaginary games if you have slightly grown up children, like spot the attractions. Keep a coloring book and colors handy for in-flight or hotel time. Apps on your smart phone can keep the children engaged with cartoons and story books. Older children are often entertained by games available on phones or tablets. This cuts the weight of luggage down while keeping the kids entertained.

30. Let the Kids Carry Their Load

A good thing is to start early sharing of responsibilities. Let your child pick a bag of his or her choice and pack it themselves. Keep tabs on what they are stuffing in their bags by asking if they will be using that item on the trip. It could start out being just an entertainment bag initially but with growing years they will learn to sort the useful from the superfluous. Children as little as four can maneuver a small trolley suitcase like a pro- their experience in pull along toys credit. If you are worried that you may be pulling it for them, you may want to start with a backpack.

31. Decide on Location for Children to Sleep

While on a trip you might not always get a crib at your destination, and carrying one will make life all the more difficult. Instead call ahead to see if there are any cribs or roll out beds for children. You may even put blankets on the floor. Weave them a story about camping and they will gladly sleep without any trouble.

32. Get Baby Products Delivered At Your Destination

If you are absolutely paranoid about not getting your favourite variety of diaper or brand of baby food, check out online stores like amazon.com for services in your destination city. You can buy things online ahead of your travel and get them delivered to your hotel upon arrival.

33. Feeding Needs Of Your Infants

If you are travelling with a breastfed infant, you save the trouble of carrying bottles and bottle sanitization kits. For special food, or medications, you may need to call ahead to make sure you have a refrigerator where you are staying.

34. Feeding Needs of Your Toddler

With the progression from infancy to toddler, their dietary requirements too evolve. You will have to pack some snacks for travelling time. Fresh fruits and vegetables can be purchased at your destination. Most of the cities you travel to in whichever part of the world, will have baby food products and formulas, available at the local drug-store or the supermarket.

35. Picking Clothes for Your Baby

Contrary to popular belief, babies can do without many changes of clothes. At the most pack 2 outfits per day. Pack mix and match type clothes for your little one as well. Pick things which are comfortable to wear and quick to dry.

36. Selecting Shoes for Your Baby

Like outfits, kids can make do with two pairs of comfortable shoes. If you can get some water resistant shoes it will be best. To expedite drying wet shoes, you can stuff newspaper in them then wrap them with newspaper and leave them to dry overnight.

37. Keep One Change of Clothes Handy

Travelling with kids can be tricky. Keep a change of clothes for the kids and mum handy in your purse or tote bag. This takes a bit of space in your hand luggage but comes extremely handy in case there are any accidents or spills.

38. Leave Behind Baby Accessories

Baby accessories like their bed, bath tub, car seat, crib etc. should be left at home. Many hotels provide a crib on request, while car seats can be borrowed from friends or rented. Babies can be given a bath in the hotel sink or even in the adult bath tub with a little bit of water. If you bring a few bath toys, they can be used in the bath, pool, and out of water. They can also be sanitized easily in the sink.

39. Carry a Small Load Of Plastic Bags

With children around there are chances of a number of soiled clothes and diapers. These plastic bags help to sort the dirt from the clean inside your big bag. These are very light weight and come in handy to other carry stuff as well at times.

Pack with a Purpose

40. Packing for Business Trips

One neutral-colored suit should suffice. It can be paired with different shirts, ties and accessories for different occasions. One pair of black suit pants could be worn with a matching jacket for the office or with a snazzy top for dinner.

41. Packing for A Cruise

Most cruises have formal dinners, and that formal dress usually takes up a lot of space. However you might find a tuxedo to rent. For women, a short black dress with multiple accessory options will do the trick.

42. Packing for A Long Trip Over Different Climates

The secret packing mantra for travel over multiple climates is layering. Layering traps air around your body creating insulation against the cold. The same light t-shirt that is comfortable in a warmer climate can be the innermost layer in a colder climate.

Reduce Some More Weight

43. Leave Precious Things At Home

Things that you would hate to lose or get damaged leave them at home. Precious jewelry, expensive gadgets or dresses, could be anything. You will not require these on your trip. Leave them at home and spare the load on your mind.

44. Send Souvenirs by Mail

If you have spent all your money on purchasing souvenirs, carrying them back in the same bag that you brought along would be difficult. Either pack everything in another bag and check it in the airport or get everything shipped to your home. Use an international carrier for a secure transit, but this could be more expensive than the checking fees at the airport.

45. Avoid Carrying Books

Books equal to weight. There are many reading apps which you can download on your smart phone or tab. Plus there are gadgets like Kindle and Nook that are thinner and lighter alternatives to your regular book.

Check, Get, Set, Check Again

46. Strategize Before Packing

Create a travel list and prepare all that you think you need to carry along. Keep everything on your bed or floor before packing and then think through once again – do I really need that? Any item that meets this question can be avoided. Remove whatever you don't really need and pack the rest.

47. Test Your Luggage

Once you have fully packed for the trip take a test trip with your luggage. Take your bags and go to town for window shopping for an hour. If you enjoy your hour long trip it is good to go, if not, go home and reduce the load some more. Repeat this test till you hit the right weight.

48. Add a Roll Of Duct Tape

You might wonder why, when this book has been talking about reducing stuff, we're suddenly asking you to pack something totally unusual. This is because when you have limited supplies, duct tape is immensely helpful for small repairs – a broken bag, leaking zip-lock bag, broken sunglasses, you name it and duct tape can fix it, temporarily.

49. List of Essential Items

Even though the emphasis is on packing light, there are things which have to be carried for any trip. Here is our list of essentials:

- Passport/Visa or any other ID

- Any other paper work that might be required on a trip like permits, hotel reservation confirmations etc.

- Medicines – all your prescription medicines and emergency kit, especially if you are travelling with children

- Medical or vaccination records

- Money in foreign currency if travelling to a different country

- Tickets- Email or Message them to your phone

50. Make the Most of Your Trip

Wherever you are going, whatever you hope to do we encourage you to embrace it whole-heartedly. Take in the scenery, the culture and above all, enjoy your time away from home.

On a long journey even a straw weighs heavy.

-Spanish Proverb

NOTES